Horace Bushnell

Present Relations of Christ with His Followers

Horace Bushnell

Present Relations of Christ with His Followers

ISBN/EAN: 9783337202392

Printed in Europe, USA, Canada, Australia, Japan

Cover: Foto ©Lupo / pixelio.de

More available books at **www.hansebooks.com**

Present Relations of Christ with His Followers

Horace Bushnell *

1892

"Ye have heard how I said unto you, I go away and come again unto you."—JOHN xiv, 28.

To go away and come again, or to go away in order to come again, would seem, taking the words at their face, to be a rather idle or unmeaning operation; but if we can get far enough into the mind of Christ to apprehend his real meaning, we shall find that he is proposing, in these words, a change of the greatest consequence—a change that is necessary to the working plan of his gospel and even to the complete value of his incarnation itself. In what sense then he is going, and in what sense he will come again, what change of relationship he will inaugurate between himself and his followers, and so

---

*"Present Relations of Christ with His Followers," in *Sermons on Christ and His Salvation* (New York: Charles Scribner's Sons, 1892), 331–50. Original version available on the Internet Archive. This version updated June 7, 2017.

1

what kind of personal relation he undertakes to hold with them now, is the subject to which I call your attention this morning, as one of intense practical interest, and even of the tenderest personal concern.

Whoever has reflected much upon the subject of the incarnation has discovered that its value depends on brevity of time, and that no such condition could be permanent, without becoming a limitation upon itself and a real hindrance to its own objects. Remaining permanently on earth in the body, Christ, plainly enough, could never have extended his rule into parts remote, or to persons debarred by distance from the external modes of access and acquaintance. The incarnation, therefore, requires shortly to be inverted. After the immense new revelation, or new salvation, of God has been accomplished, by such a manifested presence and divine life in the flesh, there needs, just as truly, to be a withdrawment from the eyes; otherwise Christ, remaining in the world and permanently fixed in it, could only gather a small circle about him, and become the center of an outward Lama worship, as restricted as the mere sight, or appearing, of the divine man-idol requires it to be.

Therefore he says—"it is expedient for you that I go away," adding the promise—"I will come to you." He means, by this, that the time has now arrived, when there must be a change of administration; when he must needs be taken away from the eyes, and begin to be set in a new spiritual relation, which permits a universal access of men to him,

332

and a universal presence of him with them—so a grand, world-wide kingdom. Saying nothing of the particular objects to be gained by his death, he could not stay here and carry on his work; he had as many friends now as he could speak with, or allow to speak with him; and if he should remain, holding fixed locality, as of a body in space, he could be the head only of a coterie, never of a kingdom. What is wanted now is an unlocalized, invisible, spiritually present, everywhere present, Saviour; such as all may know and receive, being consciously known and received by him.   333

And this will be his coming again, or his second coming—such a kind of coming as shows him bearing rule in Providence, and riding in the clouds of heaven— rolling on the changes, unfolding the destinies of time, and preparing his universal kingdom. The world, he says, seeth me no more, but ye see me; and having your spiritual eye open for this, it will be as if you saw me coming triumphantly in the clouds. This image is a well-known Eastern figure of princely pomp and majesty; they say of every great monarch, taking ascendancy, that he rides on the clouds of heaven. So, as Christ comes on, bearing sway and ruling invisible, it will be as if he were seen coming on overhead, in the clouds. And especially will this be felt when Jerusalem the Holy City is blotted out, as it were by God's hand of judgment upon it, in the conquest by Titus. By that sign goes out the old, exclusive Jew-state; and there comes in after it, now to have its place, the Christian, catholic, free state, that is to be gathered under the universal, spiritual headship of Christ. That gathering in, as in power, is to he his coming, or coming again—no bodily appearing, no visible pomp, no manifestation locally as in space; for the very thing that made it expedient for him to go away from the senses, forbids any such outward manifestation. And therefore be adds a caution, telling his disciples expressly, that his coming thus again is not to be a coming with observation. There shall be no calling "Lo, here is Christ, or lo, there," "behold he is in the desert," "behold he is in the secret chambers." The power in which he comes will be morally diffusive and secretly piercing—"as the lightning cometh out of the east and shineth even unto the west, so also shall the coming of the Son of Man be."

In all which Christ, you will perceive, is proposing to do exactly nothing which many of his disciples, specially taken by the faith of his second coming, so fervently preach and so earnestly magnify. They believe that he is to come in a body, and be visible as in body. He will of course be here or there in space, a locally present being, at some particular geographic point—Jerusalem, or London, or Rome, or going about in all places by turns. Hearing now that he is here, or there, we shall think no more of seeing him by faith, and begin to think of seeing him with our eyes. Every ship that sails will be crowded with eager multitudes pressing on to see the visible Christ. Thronging in thus, month by month, a vast seething crowd of pilgrims, curious and devout,

334

poor and rich, houseless all and hungry, trampling each other, many of them sick, not one of them in the enjoyment truly of God's peace, not one of a thousand getting near enough to see him, still fewer to hear him speak—how long will it take under such kind of experience to learn what Christ intended and the solid truth of it, when he said—"it is expedient for you that I go away," Nothing could be more inexpedient, or a profounder affliction, than a locally de-   335 scended, permanently visible, Saviour. How much better a Saviour present everywhere, and at all times; a Saviour who can say, "Lo, I am with you always," and make the promise good; one whom the heart can know, as being at rest in him, and behold, as by faith; wheeling his chariot on through all the tumults and overturnings of time, till his universal kingdom is complete.

I am well aware that our brethren, who look for Christ's visible coming, will not allow the inconveniences, or almost absurdities, I have here sketched, to be any proper results of their doctrine. "We believe," they will say, "that he will come in a spiritual body, such as he had after his resurrection, not in a coarse, material body. It will be such a body that he can be here, or there, at any given moment, hampered by no conditions of space; even as he came into the room where his disciples were gathered, when the doors were shut." But they only impose upon themselves by such a conception. If their spiritual body is to be visible, it must be as in space and outward appearing; for that is the

condition of all visibility. And then we have a
flitting Saviour, breaking out here or there, at what
time, or on what occasion, no mortal can guess. And
the result will be that they are in a worse torment
than they would be, if he were established in some
known locality. Going after their eyes, they are
taken off from all faith, and where their eyes shall
find him they know not.

Pardon me then if I suggest the suspicion that
they are more carnal in their expectation than they
know. If it is so much better to have a visible Saviour,
are they not more weary of faith than they should be,
and secretly longing, catching at straws of prophecy,
to get away from it? There is nothing, I must frankly
say, that would be so nearly a dead loss of Christ to
any disciple who knows him in the dear companionship of faith, as to have him come in visible show;
either setting up his reign at some geographic point,
or reigning aerially, in some flitting and cursitating
manner which can not be traced. How beautifully
accessible is he now everywhere, present to every
heart that loves him; consciously dear, as friend, consoler, guide, and stay, in all conditions; close at hand
in every sinking ship in the uttermost parts of the
sea; the sweet joy of dungeons under ground, where
there is no light to see him in a body; immediately
and all-diffusively present, to comfort every sorrow,
support every persecution, and even to turn away
the tempting thought before it comes. A Saviour in
the body and before the eyes can serve no such of-
fices. None can find him, but them that come in his

336

way, or chance to spy him with their eyes.

We have no want then of a locally related, that is of a bodily resident Saviour; we perceive, without difficulty, the expediency of which Christ speaks, that he should go away and not continue the incarnate, or visible state, longer than to serve the particular objects for which he assumed that state. But he gives us to understand, that he is not going to be taken utterly away in the proposed removal,   337 but rather to be as much closer to his disciples as he can be, when all conditions of time and space are cast off. And accordingly the question rises at this point, how is Christ related now to the knowledge and friendship of his people? "Ye have heard how I said unto you I go away and come again unto you." And again—"I wilt not leave you comfortless, I will come to you." And again—"but ye see me." And again—"Lo, I am with you always." He evidently means to put himself thus in a practically close and dear relation with his people— what is that relation? how set open? how maintained?

Obviously what we want ourselves, is to be somehow with him, and to know that he is with us. We want a social, consciously open state with him, as real as if he were with us bodily, and as diffusive as if he were everywhere; thus to have a personal enjoyment of him, and rest in the felt sympathies of his personal companionship. This, too, exactly is what he means to allow us; not in the external way, but in a way more immediate, and blessed, and evident, and as much more beneficial. If we

had him with us in the external way, as his own
disciples had, when they journeyed, and talked, and
eat, and slept, in his company, we should be living
altogether in our eyes, and not in any way of mental
realization. And, as a result, we should not be raised
and exalted in spiritual force, or character, as we
specially need to be. What we want, therefore, is to
have a knowledge of him, and presence and society
with him, that we can carry with us, and have as
338   the secret joy, and strength, and conscious blessing
of our inmost life itself; that we may see him, when
we are blind and can see nothing with our eyes; that
we may hear him speak, when we are deaf and can
hear nothing with our ears; that we may walk with
him, when we can not walk at all; sit in heavenly
places with him, when we can not sit at all; rise with
him when he rises, reign with him when he reigns;
never away from him, even when beyond the sea, or
passing through the valley of the shadow of death.

Now it is just this relation that he undertakes to
fill, when he goes away. Being himself a Comforter,
[Paraclete,] for this is the word translated Advocate,
he promises "another Comforter;" that is, in some
proper sense, another self. Indeed, he really calls
the Comforter promised, another self; for he says
expressly, in this very connection—"Even the Spirit
of truth, whom the world can not receive because it
seeth him not; neither knoweth him, but ye know
him; for he dwelleth with you and shall be in you;"
striking directly into the first person, to say the same
thing over again, as relating to himself—"Yet a lit-

tle while and the world seeth me no more, but ye see me; because I live, ye shall live also. At that day ye shall know that I am in my Father, and ye in me, and I in you." And then, to be still more explicit, he gives the promise, that whosoever of his followers follows faithfully, keeping his commandments, shall have the immediate manifestation always of his presence—"I will manifest myself onto him,"—"If a man love me he will keep my words, and my Father 339 will love him, and we will come unto him and make our abode with him."

The great change of administration thus to be introduced, by the going away and coming again, includes several points that require to be distinctly noted.

1. That Christ now institutes such a relationship between him and his followers, that they can know him when the world can not. Before this, the world had known him just as his disciples had, seeing him with their eyes, hearing his doctrine, observing his miracles, but flow he is to be withdrawn, so that only they shall see him—"the world seeth him not." As being rational persons, they may recollect him, they may read other men's recollections of him, but his presence they will not discern, he is not manifest unto them, but only to his followers. He that loveth knoweth God, and he only.

2. It is a point included that the new presence, or social relationship, is to be effected and maintained by the Holy Spirit, the Comforter. And he it is that Christ, in the promise, calls so freely himself.

The New Testament writings are not delicate in maintaining any particular formula, or scheme of personality, as regards the distributions of Trinity. They call the Spirit "the Spirit of Christ." They say, "God hath sent the Spirit of his Son into your hearts." They speak of "the supply of the Spirit of Jesus Christ." They speak also of "the law of the Spirit of life in Christ Jesus." They say, "the Lord [Christ] is that Spirit." Christ also is shown, more than once, fulfilling the official functions of the Spirit; as in Paul's conversion, where the invisible Christ, that is the Spirit, says "I am Jesus of Nazareth whom thou persecutest;" or again, when Paul him self describes his conversion by saying, "when it pleased God to reveal his Son in me." No theologic scruples are felt in such free modes of expression, and indeed there never should be; for to every one but the strict tritheist, Christ must, in some sense, be the Spirit, and the Spirit, Christ. And when Christ calls the Comforter he promises, himself he gives precisely the best and truest representation of the Spirit, in his new office, possible to be given. It is to be as if the disincarnated soul, or person of Christ, were now to go away and return as a universal Spirit invisible; in that form "to abide forever." And the beauty of the conception is, that the Spirit is to be no mere impersonal effluence, or influence, but to be with us in the very feeling and charity of Jesus. All the fullness of Christ is in him; the gentleness, the patience, the tenderness, the self-sacrifice; all that makes Jesus himself such a power of personal

340

mastery in us. He is to be with us in Christ's name as a being with a heart, nay, to be the heart itself that was beating in the Son of Mary. All the charities, and even the blessed humanities of Jesus are to be in him, and, in fact, to be ministered socially, and socially manifested by him; even as Christ expressly declared—"He shall glorify me; for he shall receive of mine and show it unto you." This inward showing is, in fact, the virtuality of Christ. He will be to the soul all that Christ himself would 341 wish to be; for he loves the world with Christ's own love. He will be as forgiving as Christ in his passion, as tenderly burdened as Christ in his agony, as really present to physical suffering, as truly a Comforter to all the shapes of human sorrow. All which Christ outwardly expressed, he will inwardly show.

3. In this coming again of Christ by the Spirit, there is included also the fact that he will be known by the disciple, not only socially, but as the Christ, in such a way as to put us in a personal relationship with him, even as his own disciples were in their outward society with him. "Ye shall know that I am in the Father, and ye in me, and I in you." "But ye know him," "But ye see me," Many persons appear to suppose that the Holy Spirit works in a manner back of all consciousness, and that there is even a kind of extravagance in the disciple who presumes to know him. And so it really is, if the conception is that he knows him by sensation, or by inward phantasy. But what means the apostle when he says—"the Spirit itself beareth witness with our Spirit that we are the

children of God"? That bearing witness with imports some kind of inward society, or interchange, in which a divine testimony flows into human impression, or conviction, else it imports nothing. The real Christian fact in regard to this very important subject appears to be, that the Holy Spirit, or Spirit of Christ, though not felt by sensation, or beheld by mental vision, is yet revealed, back of all perception, in the consciousness. We are made originally to be

342 conscious of God, just as we are of ourselves, and know him by that immediate light. This is our normal state and it is now so far restored. Our finite being was to be complete in the infinite, and apart from that, could only be a poor dead limb, or broken fragment, worthless to itself. And this accordingly is the wonder of a true religious experience begun, that the soul, awakened to the consciousness of God, not knowing how, has a certain mysterious feeling of otherness imparted, which is somehow a new element to it—a pure, inwardly glorious, free element. By and by it gets acquainted with the new and glorious incoming, and dares to say, it is Christ, it is God. A whole side of the nature turning Godward thus, and before closed, is now open, and the man is even more impressively conscious at times of the divine movement in his feeling, than of his own. And this fulfills the promise—" I will manifest myself unto him." A promise which Paul bravely answers, when he says, out of his own conscious experience—" Christ liveth in me,"—"who loved me and gave himself for me."

Here then is the relationship we seek—Christ is so related now, to the soul of them that receive him, that he is present with them in all places, at all times, bearing witness with their spirit, in guidance and holy society; a friend, a consoler, a glorious illuminator, all that he would or could be, if we had him each to him self in outward company. Yes, and he is more than this; for if we simply had him in such outward company, the contrast perceived would be even mortifying and oppressive; but now,   343
as be comes up from within, through our personal consciousness itself, we are raised in dignity, and have him as the sense of a new and nobler self unfolded in us. O, what a footing is this for a mortal creature to occupy, an open relationship with Christ and God, in which it shall receive just all which it wants, being consciously girded with strength for whatever it has to do, patience for suffering, wisdom for guidance. His very nature is penetrated by a higher nature, and, being spirit to Spirit, he moves in the liberty of that superior impulse and advisement His relationship to Christ is that of the branch to the vine, and the presence that he has with Christ is immediate, vital, and if he will suffer it, perpetual. Its whole gospel in one view it has in the promise—"Lo, I am with you always, even to the end of the world."

But there is a different conception of this whole matter, which I must briefly notice. Many persons appear to assume, that we have, and can have, no relations to Christ, more immediate than those

which we have through language and the understanding. The Spirit, they say, works by truth, and
only as the truth gets power in our thoughts and
choices. Their conception is that we have nothing
to do with God, except as we get hold of notions, or
notional truths, concerning him—reported facts, for
example, and teachings, and doctrinal deductions.
Undoubtedly we are to have this notional furniture
in the understanding, but it is never to be a fence
between us and God, requiring us to know him only
344   at second hand, as we know China by the report of
the geographers. We are still to know God, or Christ,
by our immediate experience; nay, to know him as
we know ourselves, by consciousness. It is useful
for us to know ourselves scientifically, intellectually,
reflectively; but this kind of artificial self-knowledge
is not enough. Some of us, in that way, would
scarcely know ourselves at all, and none of us more
than partially, intermittently, and in spots. We want
to know ourselves all the while, and without study,
so as to be all the while possessing and going along
with ourselves, and therefore we are gifted with
an immediate consciousness of ourselves. But we
want, just as much, to know God by this immediate
and perpetual knowledge; for apart from God we
are nothing, we do not even half exist. Our finite existence becomes complete existence, only as we are
complete in him, and this we can not be, save as he
is manifested, or participated, by our consciousness.
Thus we might have our advantage in a notional,
or scientific conception of the atmosphere, but if we

could breathe only by such scientific self-regulation, many of us would stop breathing entirely, and all of us would be gasping for air a great part of the time; what we want is a continual fanning of the breath that shall keep the air at work, feeding our life all the time, without intermission, and without any kind of notional self-regulation. So, too, we want a perpetual inbreathing of God, a witnessing of the divine Spirit with our spirit, else our very nature is abortive and worthless. It is not enough that we have notions, or doctrines, of God, which we may use, or apply, to obtain flavors of good effect through   345 such media—we want the immediate manifestation of God himself. And then, lest we should sink away into the abysses and trances of contemplation, with Plotinus and others who struggle out vaguely into and after the infinite, we have the infinite humanly personated in Christ; so that, instead of wandering off into any abysses at all, we simply let the Son of Man be God in our feeling, and fashion us in the molds of his own humanly divine excellence. Christ we say liveth in us; and therefore by the faith of the Son of God, we live.

But is not this a kind of mysticism, some will ask, better therefore to be avoided than received ? I hardly know what is definitely meant by the question; unless perhaps it be that a word is wanted that will serve the uses of a stigma. A great many will begin to suspect some kind of mysticism, just because they are mystified, or misted, and see things only in a fog of obscurity. But if this be mysticism, nothing is plainer than that Christ is the original teacher of it, and his two disciples, John and Paul, specially abundant teachers of it after him. Every man is a mystic in the same way, who believes that Christ is the Life—in such a sense the life that he truly liveth in his followers, and giveth them to live by him, God as the Life, the all-quickener, the all-mover and sustainer, the inward glory and bliss of souls—this may be set down as a thing too high to be any but a mystical notion. And yet all highest things are apt to be most rational, and, at bottom, most credible. What can be more rational, in fact, than to think that God will give us most certainly what is most wanted—water, and light, and air, and yet more freely, Himself? He will not put us off to know only things about him, truths, notions, items of feet, but will give us to know Himself. And since all souls are dark, living only to grope, without him—poor, blind pilgrims, straying on the shores of eternity—what will he do, what, in all true reason, must he do, but make himself the true sunrising to them, and the conscious revelation of their inward day.

346

Our answer then to the question what are Christ's present relations to his followers? is that he is present to them as he is not, and can not be to the world; present as an all-permeating Spirit; present as the all-quickening Life; consciously, socially present; so that no explorations of science, or debates of reason are wanted to find him, no going over the sea to bring him back, or up into heaven to bring him down; because he is already present, always present, in the mouth and in the heart. In this manner he will be revealed in all men, waits to be revealed in all, if only they will suffer it. Tho word for every loving, trusting heart is, "I will come unto you, I will be manifest in you. Lo, I will be with you always."

But the answer at which we thus arrive is a purely spiritual answer, you perceive, one that is real and true only as it is opened to faith, and experimentally proved. But all such spiritualities waver and flicker; we are too much in the senses to hold them constantly and evenly enough to rest in them. Therefore to keep us in the range of this 347 relationship, God has contrived to fasten us in the sense of it, and make it good, by two fixed, partly outward institutes, that are to stand as forts, or fortresses, in the foreground of it; viz., by the church and by the sacraments.

"Behold the kingdom of God is within you," says the Saviour, meaning that he will be there, and there will have his reign. But he also lays the foundations of a great, perpetual, visible institute, that he names the church, calling it to be the light of the world, even as he, in the body, was the light of the world himself, and because he is now, in the Spirit, to be entered into and fill the body of the church with light. His apostle calls it too "the pillar and ground of the truth," because it is to be that corporate body that never dies, receiving the written word as a deposit

and trust for all ages to come, and becoming itself
a living epistle, answering faithfully to it, and shed-
ding, from its own luminous property, a perpetual
light of interpretation upon it. Of this body, called
the church, he is to be the Head himself, and all the
members joined together in him, are to be so related
to him as to make a virtually real, and perpetually
diffusive, incarnation of him in the world. While,
therefore, it was expedient for him to go away as the
Son of Man, or of Mary, it was yet to be found, as he
comes again by revelation to the consciousness of his
disciples, that he is again taking body, in fact, for all
time, in them; so to be manifested organically, and,
as it were, instituted in their undying and corporate
348   membership—"Head over all things to the church
which is his body, the fullness of him that filleth all
in all." The members are to know him personally,
each in his own immediate life, and then they are to
know him again even the more firmly, that they are
consciously instituted and framed into body by his
life. It is to be as if their divine consciousness itself
were certified, and sealed, and made visible, by its
own organizing power—that power which ages and
times can not weaken, which outlives the kingdoms
and their persecutions, and defies the gates of hell.
"From whence the whole body, fitly joined together
and compacted by that which every joint supplieth,
according to the effectual working in the measure of
every part, maketh increase of the body unto the ed-
ifying of itself in love," What solidity is there now in
such a relation to Christ! Spiritual as the relation is, it

is yet even more intellectually fixed, and carries better evidence, than Christ in the body was ever able to give his followers.

But the spiritualities of the relation Christ maintains with his disciples were to be settled and fortified by still another institute; I mean the sacraments, and especially the sacrament of the Holy Supper. The very object of the supper appears to be the settlement, and practical, or experimental, certification of that revelation to consciousness, of which we have been speaking. "This is my body, take and eat." "This is my blood, drink ye all of it." And this, to establish, as by institute, the fact that Christ here present, is to be communicated and received, as by nutrition, or as life. And this is what is meant by discerning his body, and the showing 349 forth of his death; for there is to be an accepting, in the partaker, of his here represented embodiment, and a confession of trust in his death, to which he will, by these instituted symbols and pledges, be inwardly discovered, as certainly and as often as the rite is duly observed. When, therefore, he says, "this do in remembrance of me," we are not to take his words in the lightest, shallowest possible meaning, as if he were only giving us a mnemonic to refresh our memories, but in the deepest and most sacredly inward sense; viz., that he is giving it to us here, to receive the dearest hospitality, the communion of bis own divine Life, All that famous discourse of his about the bread and the blood, in the 6th chapter of John, is but the fit opening of his meaning. "I am

the bread of life—the living bread that came down
from heaven—if any man eat of this bread he shall
live forever. My flesh is meat indeed, and my blood
is drink indeed. Except ye eat the flesh of the Son of
Man and drink his blood, ye have no life in you."

And this exactly is the great institute of the supper. Christ engages to be present in it, by a most real
presence, without a miracle of transubstantiation; so
that when we come to offer to him ourselves, and
open our inmost receptivities to the appropriation of
his presence, it is no vague, volunteer, possibly pre-
sumptuous thing that we do, as if venturing on some
almost aerial flight, in the way of coming unto God,
but we have the grace by institution, firmly pledged,
and given, as it were, by routine. Here is Christ to be
communicated. Here are we to commune. There is
350   no miracle, but what is a great deal better, viz., life;
community of life with Christ and God. What we get
in the conscious revelation of his Spirit, we here receive by an outward and perpetually instituted dis-
pensation. And we have this communion also with
each other as with Christ; because he is the common
life, which is endeavoring always a common growth
in the members.

O, that we might receive this supper to-day, my
brethren, according to its true meaning, and eat and
drink worthily. Take it as no mere commemorative
ceremony over Christ dead, but as the appointed
vehicle of Christ living, and in you to live. Come
not here to be sad and sit mourning for your Master's body, like the women weeping for Tammuz.

Consider, above all, this, that Christ, once dead, is here alive, that he may here dispense himself to you. Blessed is the heart that shall be fully opened to him. Be that true, as it may be, of you all; that you may go forth loving one another as you love your Master, and shining without, by the light he gives you within. Neither forget how that open, dear relation of spirit with him, of which we have been speaking, is here sanctioned publicly for you, and sanctified before you, even as by an institute of God. As he has gone away, so believe, henceforth and always, that he has come again. Count this coming in the Spirit to be with you, dearer than even outward society with him would be, such as his disciples had at the first; and expect to be always with him in this manner, in the closest, most immediate knowledge; even as he said himself—BUT YE SEE ME.

www.ingramcontent.com/pod-product-compliance
Lightning Source LLC
Chambersburg PA
CBHW031157090426
42738CB00008B/1373